THE UNIVERSE

SEYMOUR SIMON

MORROW JUNIOR BOOKS
New York

PHOTO AND ART CREDITS
Permission to use the following photographs is gratefully acknowledged:
page 5: National Optical Astronomy Observatories; pages 7, 24, 31: NRAO/NSS;
page 8: Chris Butler/Science Photo Library; page 11: Royal Observatory, Edinburgh/AATB/Science Photo Library;
page 15: Mark McCaughrean (Max-Planck-Institute for Astronomy), C. Robert O'Dell (Rice University), and NASA;
page 16: Jeff Hester and Paul Scowen (Arizona State University) and NASA; page 19: Raghvendra Sahai and
John Trauger (JPL), the SFPC2 Science Team, and NASA; page 21: C. Robert O'Dell and Kerry P. Handron
(Rice University) and NASA; pages 22–23: David A. Hardy/Science Photo Library;
page 27: Robert Williams and the Hubble Deep Field Team (STScI) and NASA; page 29: Berry/STSCI;
page 32: M. Rich (Columbia University), W. Freedman (Carnegie Observatories), and NASA.
Front jacket photograph © Jeff Hester and Paul Scowen (Arizona State University) and NASA;
back jacket photograph © NRAO/NSS.
Art on pages 12–13 by Ann Neumann.

The text type is 18–point Garamond Book.

Published by Morrow Junior Books
a division of William Morrow and Company, Inc.
1350 Avenue of the Americas, New York, NY 10019
http://www.williammorrow.com

Printed in Singapore at Tien Wah Press.

1 2 3 4 5 6 7 8 9 10

Library of Congress Cataloging-in-Publication Data
Simon, Seymour.
The universe/Seymour Simon.
p. cm.
Summary: Describes the expansion of the universe as a result of the Big Bang.
ISBN 0-688-15301-1 (trade)—ISBN 0-688-15302-X (library)
1. Cosmology—Juvenile literature.   [1. Cosmology.]   I. Title.
QB983.S66 1998   523-dc21   97-20489   CIP AC

To Michael, Debra, and Chloe

The universe is everything that exists, now and in the past. It includes the book you are reading and the ground beneath your feet, the animals and plants, oceans and continents, planets, stars, and galaxies, and the vast reaches of space. You are truly part of the universe. Every atom, every particle within you, is billions of years old.

If you wanted to write your complete address on a letter, to show where you live, it might look like this:

Your name

Street, city or town, zip code, country

Planet Earth

Solar System

Milky Way Galaxy

The Universe

There's no zip code for the universe, of course, but if there was one, it might be ∞, which is the symbol for infinity.

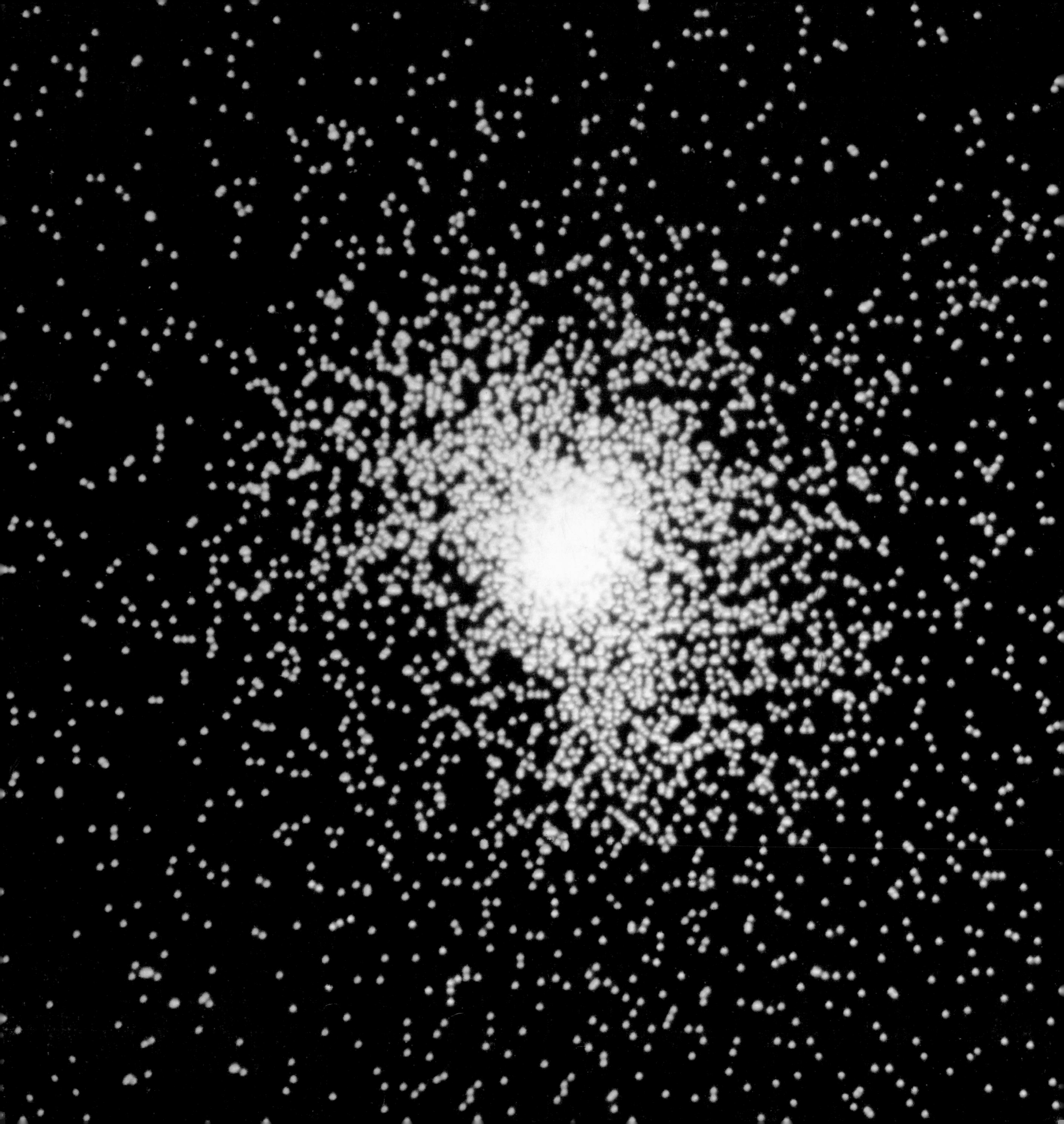

In the beginning, there was no space and no time. Everything was squeezed together under incredibly high pressure and temperature. Then, more than ten billion years ago, the universe suddenly exploded into being. Scientists call this the Big Bang. Matter formed and was carried outward by the blast, and time as we know it began.

After the explosion, the universe was small and very hot. Then as the universe expanded, it cooled, and small particles of matter combined to form hydrogen and helium gases. Over billions of years these cooling gases produced all of the universe and all of us.

Even today we can see galaxies exploding with energy produced by the Big Bang. This computer-enhanced photo shows radio waves streaming out from a hot spot in a cosmic jet of gases shooting out from a distant galaxy.

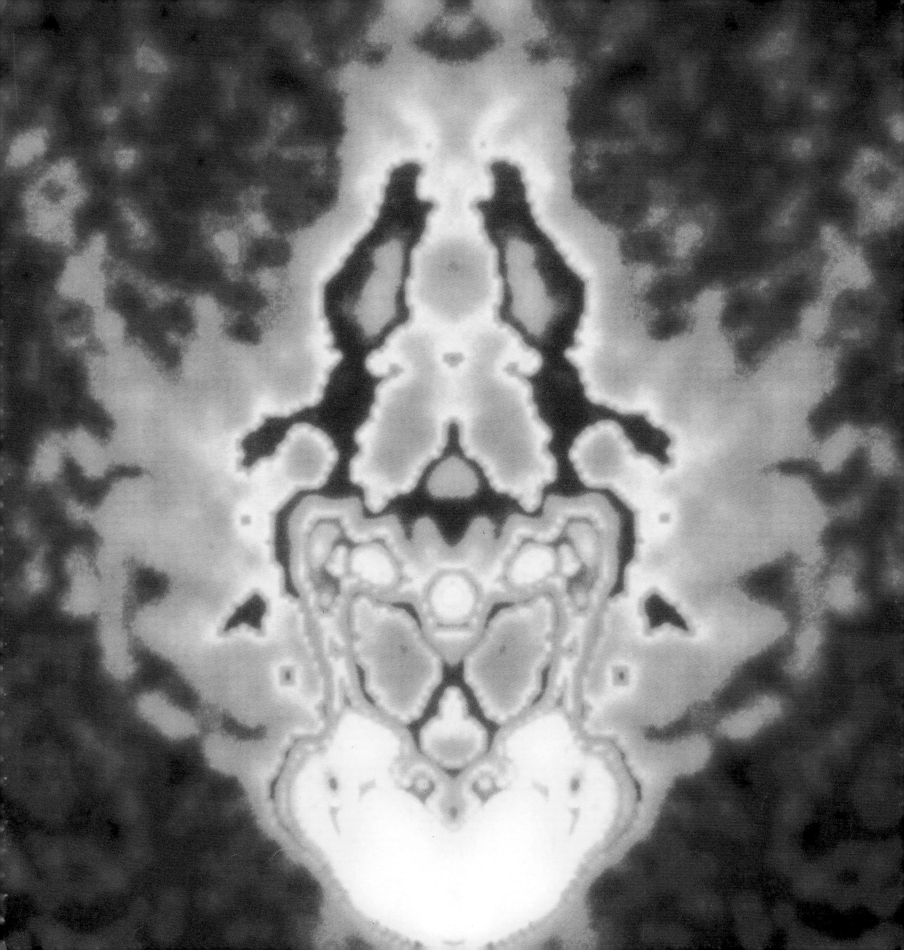

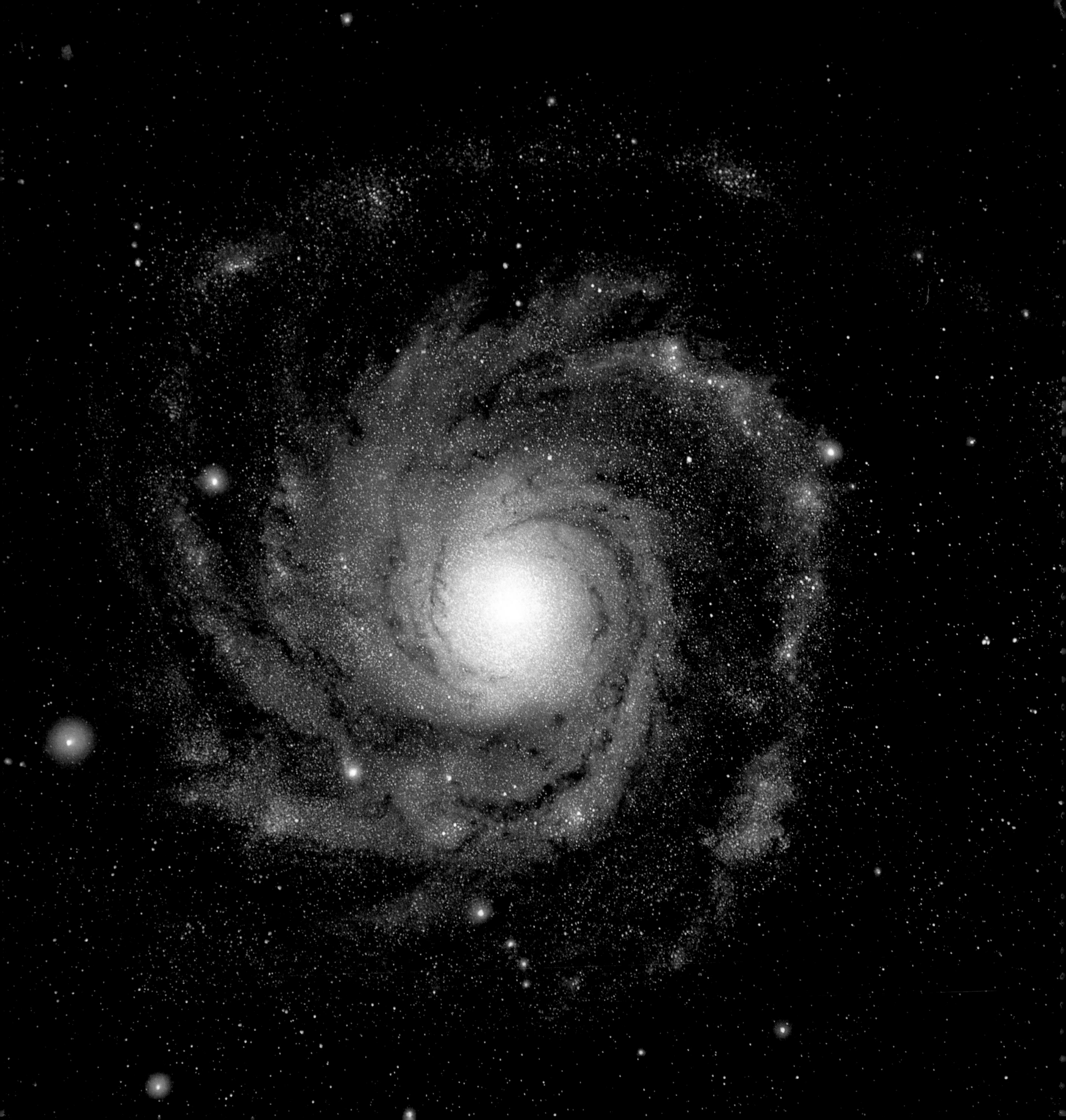

The universe is still expanding as a result of the Big Bang. Galaxies speed away from one another, some traveling thousands of miles per second.

Will the universe continue to expand forever? In billions of years will the stars and galaxies begin to blink out as they lose energy? Will only dying stars and galaxies be left, surrounded by empty space? Perhaps the universe will slow down and finally stop expanding. Will it then begin to pull back together, to end in a Big Crunch and another Big Bang?

From Earth we can look into space and study the universe with telescopes and other instruments. The Moon is Earth's nearest neighbor in space, only about a quarter of a million miles away. That's very close in space, almost next door. Still, it's very far away compared to the distance between places on Earth's surface. You'd have to travel around the Earth ten times in order to match the distance from the Earth to the Moon. The Sun, the closest star to us, is over four hundred times farther away from us than the Moon is—about ninety-three million miles.

The nearest star after our Sun is much farther away than that. But measuring the distance between stars and planets in miles is like measuring the distance around the world in inches. We measure the distance to the stars in light-years: the distance that light travels in one year, which is close to six *trillion* miles. A spaceship speeding at ten miles per second would still take more than seventy thousand *years* to get to Alpha Centauri, the nearest star after the Sun—a distance of 4.3 light-years, or twenty-five trillion miles.

About four-and-a-half billion years ago, the Sun and the planets formed from a swirling disk of dust, ice, and gas in space. The particles slowly pulled together, and the Sun was born first, in the center of the disk. The rest of the material then formed into the planets.

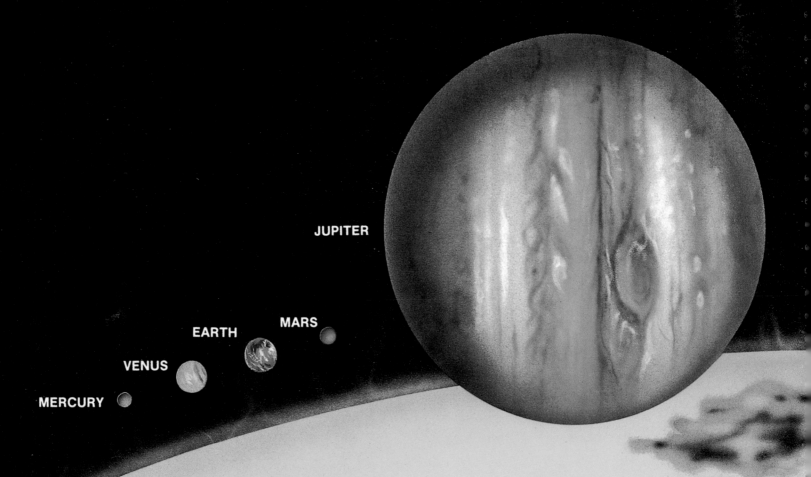

JUPITER

MARS

EARTH

VENUS

MERCURY

SUNSPOTS

SUN

Mercury, Venus, Earth, and Mars are closest to the Sun and are called the inner planets. These rocky planets are much smaller than the giant outer planets: Jupiter, Saturn, Uranus, and Neptune, which are made mostly of gases. Pluto, the outermost and smallest of the planets, is 3.6 billion miles from the Sun.

SATURN

URANUS

NEPTUNE

● PLUTO

For many years, our Solar System was the only one we had ever seen. But in recent years, scientists using new instruments began to observe what looked like other solar systems in the making. These are four images of gas-and-dust disks forming around young stars. The disks range in size from about two to eight times the diameter of our Solar System. The glow in the center of each disk is a newly formed star, about one million years old.

The disks do not mean, for certain, that planets will form. But the building blocks for planets are there. Now that they know so many young stars have planetary disks, scientists feel more optimistic about the possibility of locating other solar systems.

Finding individual planets is more challenging than finding planetary disks, because a single planet is much smaller and more compact than a whole solar system in the making. Still, we have discovered more planets around distant stars than in our own Solar System.

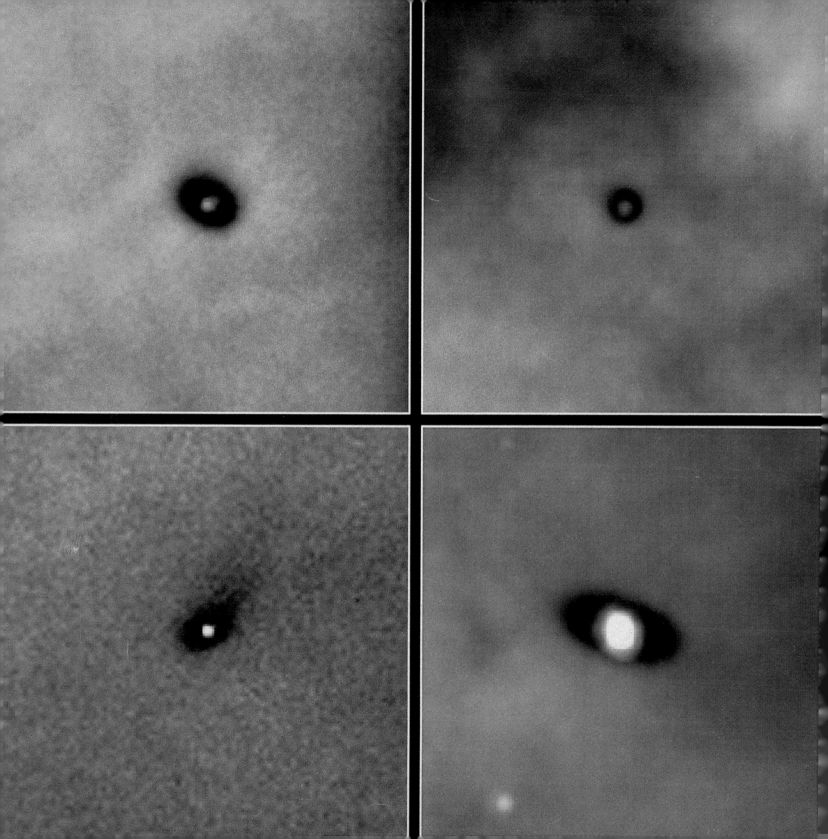

All stars are born within nebulas, which are eerie dark clouds of hydrogen gas and dust. Stars are not born singly but in groups or clusters. Usually each star grows at a different speed, and most clusters finally drift apart. Some of the young stars are ten thousand times brighter than our Sun is now.

This photo of the Eagle Nebula—also called M-16—was taken by the Hubble Space Telescope in 1995. The Eagle Nebula is in a nearby star-forming region of the Milky Way Galaxy. It is about seven thousand light-years away from Earth. The new stars are the bright lights inside the fingerlike bulges at the top of the nebula. Each "fingertip" is tens of billions of miles across—larger than our entire Solar System.

When stars get older, they cool off, swell up one hundred times larger, and turn red. These aging stars are called red giants. The red giants become very active, blowing off violent gusts of hot gas from their surfaces into space. When a red giant has shed its outer layers, the hot core within the star makes the surrounding cloud of gases glow. This cloud is called a planetary nebula because early astronomers thought its shape and color looked like a planet.

Planetary nebulas come in a variety of shapes: from narrow jets of exploding gases to peanut-shaped clouds to bright globes surrounding stars. This Hubble Space Telescope image of a cosmic bubble is an hourglass-shaped planetary nebula around a distant star. The red rings are nitrogen gases. The potato-shaped inner rings of green and blue are hydrogen and oxygen. The hot star that gave birth to the nebula is a bit off center, to the left of the inner blue ring.

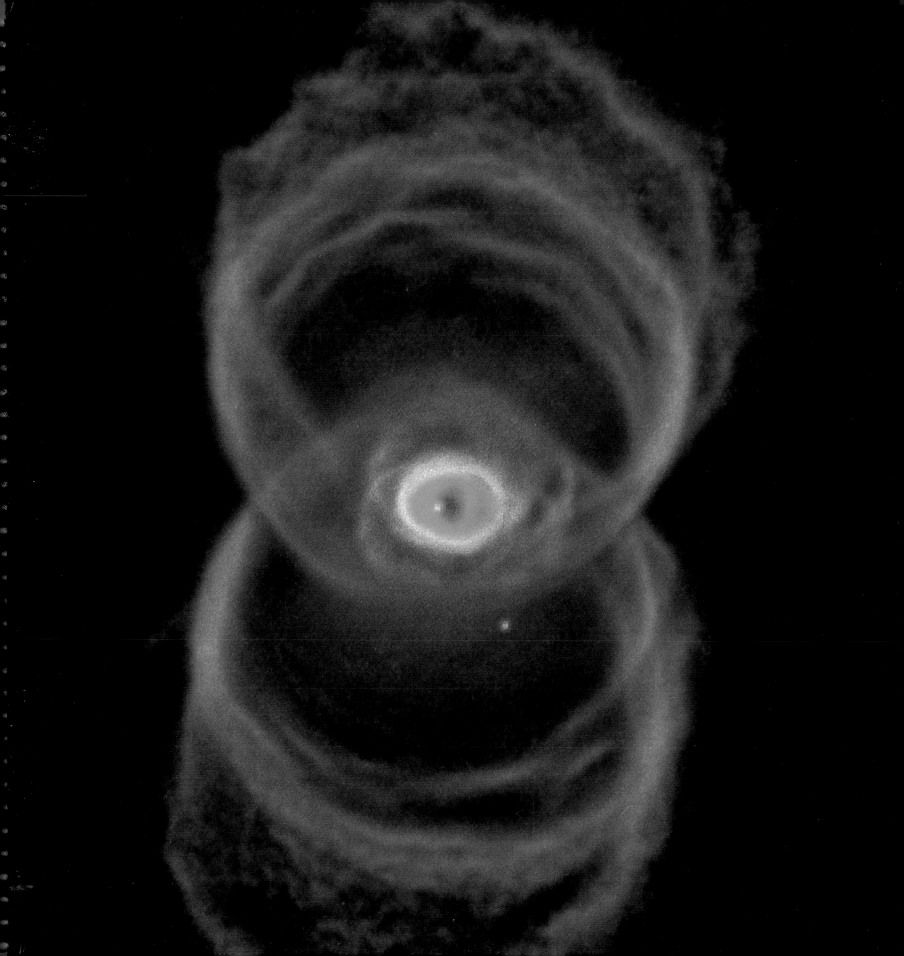

What look like spaceships from a science fiction movie are really the result of a dying star's final outbursts. These mysterious "space pods" are gigantic tadpole-shaped clumps of gas, each several billion miles across, twice the size of our Solar System. The cometlike tails fan out around the central star like the spokes on a wheel.

No one knows what will happen to the pods. Perhaps they will expand and disappear within a few hundred thousand years. Or perhaps the dust particles inside each gas ball will collide and stick together. Planets the size of Earth, but frigid and icy like the planet Pluto, might form over time. Thousands of these icy worlds might escape the dead star and roam the dark space between the stars forever.

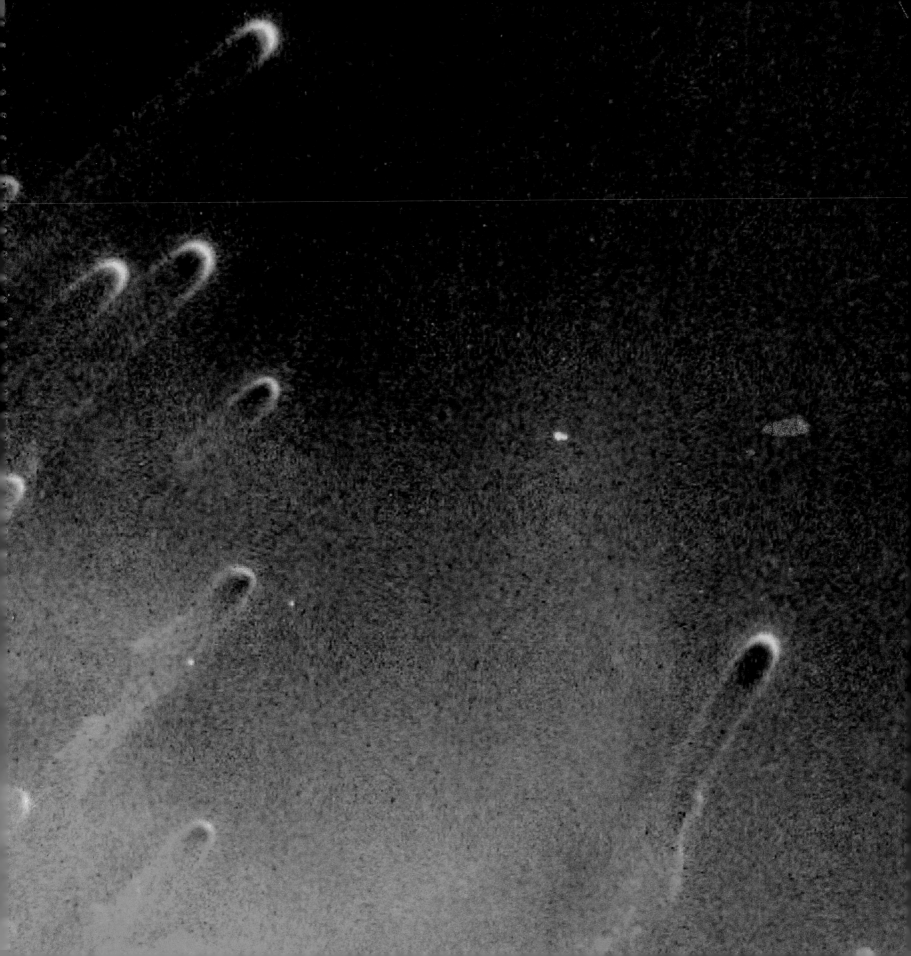

Our Sun is just one of about two hundred billion stars in the Milky Way Galaxy, a vast spiral of stars about one hundred thousand light-years across. Viewed from the side, it looks like a lens, with a thick bright center of stars and flattened edges. All the stars we see in the night sky are in our galaxy. Other galaxies are much too distant for us to see their individual stars.

Our Solar System is about thirty thousand light-years away from the center of the Milky Way. The central galaxy is much more crowded than our lonely part of space. In one star cluster near the center of the Milky Way, there are one hundred thousand stars in one cubic light-year. But in our remote corner of the galaxy, there are no stars within four light-years of our Solar System.

This is a radio photo of a star called Sagittarius A*, near the center of the Milky Way. Hidden someplace within this photo, there might be an enormous black hole marking the true center of our galaxy.

Scientists class galaxies by their shape. There are four main types of galaxies: spirals, ellipticals, barred spirals, and irregular-shaped galaxies. Spirals are disk-shaped, with older stars in the center and newer stars in the arms. Ellipticals are the most common and are shaped like balls or eggs. They contain mostly old stars. Barred spirals are spirals whose central stars form a bar. Irregulars are the rarest and do not fit any known pattern.

Many galaxies in space are so distant that their light fades out before it reaches the Earth, and they can only be seen with radio telescopes. This radio image of a large elliptical galaxy called Fornax A is in the center of a distant cluster of galaxies. The central bright white region shines with the light of more than ten billion stars. Fornax A is so huge that it is swallowing nearby galaxies. The small spiral galaxy just above Fornax A may soon be captured.

Scientists think that there are at least one hundred billion galaxies in the universe, and each galaxy contains about one hundred billion stars. There are more stars in the universe than there are grains of sand on all the beaches in the world.

This photo is the deepest view of the universe ever seen through a telescope. It covers a speck of the sky the size of a dime seen from seventy-five feet away. Gazing into this small spot with a high-powered telescope, scientists discovered fifteen hundred galaxies in different stages of their lives. From Earth, some of these galaxies are as faint as a flashlight on the Moon would be.

Looking at distant galaxies in the universe with a telescope is like using a time machine to peer into the past. Light from the dimmest galaxies shown here has taken ten billion years to reach us, beginning its journey only a few billion years after the birth of the universe in the Big Bang.

Among the strangest objects in the universe are black holes. A black hole is a region of space where matter is squeezed together so tightly and the pull of its gravity is so powerful that nothing can escape from it, not even light. It is impossible to see a black hole, but we can see vast amounts of matter being sucked into the hole, never to return. Black holes seem to come in two sizes: small and superlarge. The small ones are formed when stars collapse and are only a few miles in diameter. Most we cannot detect.

Scientists think that the superlarge black holes are probably at the center of most galaxies. This drawing shows a spiral of dust and gases eight hundred light-years wide being sucked into a giant black hole in the center of a nearby galaxy. The black hole contains more than one billion times the amount of matter in our Sun, all packed tightly together.

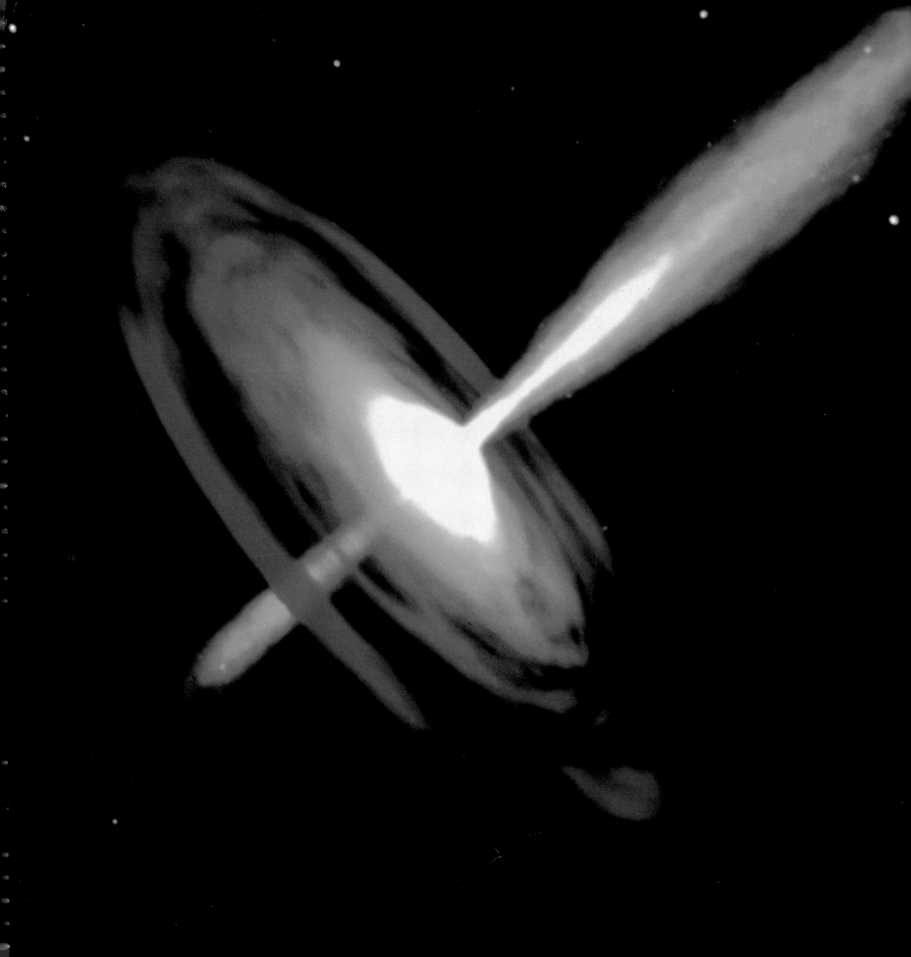

These discoveries have led to new mysteries: Does every galaxy have a black hole at its center? If there's a black hole in a galaxy, does that mean that all the stars in the galaxy will eventually disappear inside it? What starts a black hole, and does it ever end?

Quasars are as mysterious as black holes. Before stars vanish into a black hole, they give off energy in a burst of light and radio waves. This outpouring of energy is called a quasar. About the size of our Solar System, quasars contain the mass of more than a million Suns. Yet they pour out one hundred to one thousand times as much light as an entire *galaxy* of one hundred billion stars.

Quasars are the most distant objects in the universe that astronomers are able to view with optical telescopes. They are so bright they are like distant headlights illuminating all the material along the path of their light to us. We see quasars as they were ten or more billion years ago, only a billion years after the Big Bang. This photo combines a telescope view of a nearby galaxy and a much more distant radio-telescope view of a quasar.

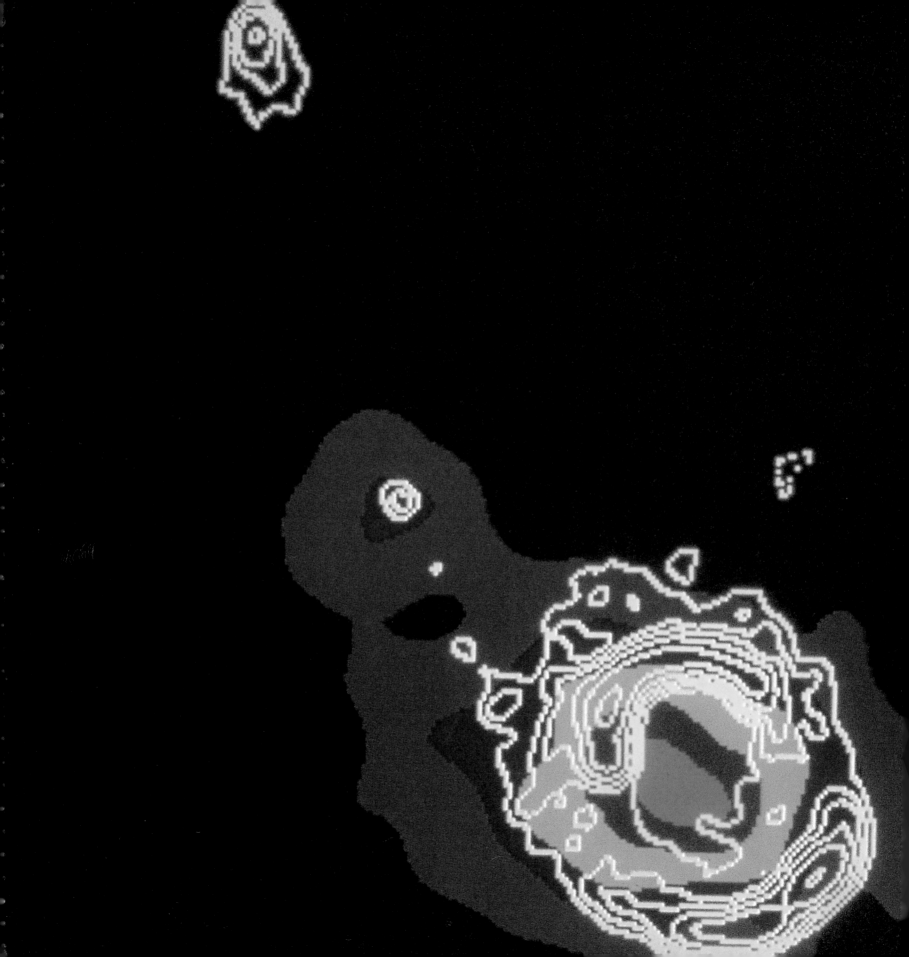

Does life exist on Earth-like planets in distant solar systems? Will the universe expand forever or finally stop and then collapse into a gigantic black hole? Searching for answers about the universe is like exploring a dark, mysterious ocean without being able to leave the shore. But with the Hubble Space Telescope and other new methods of gathering information, we are just at the beginning of a golden age of discovery. No one knows what fantastic places we will see.